Praise for *A Short Sound in the Silence:*

"It's so good, my dude."

-Rose Watson

"It's ok, I guess."

-Ellie Gray

"That's nice, Jared."

-My Mom

"You published a book?"

-Everyone Else

A SHORT SOUND IN THE SILENCE

An Eco-Critical Anthology

by Jared De Roo

With Contributions from
Rose Watson and Savannah McClellan

A Short Sound in the Silence by Jared De Roo

Published by Jared De Roo

© 2017 Jared De Roo

Cover by Jared De Roo

Includes works by Rose Watson and Savannah McClellan

ISBN-13: 978-1979930468

ISBN-10: 1979930465

For Dr. Whitson, Dr. Jarvis, and Dustin Wyse-Fisher,

without whom this would not have been possible.

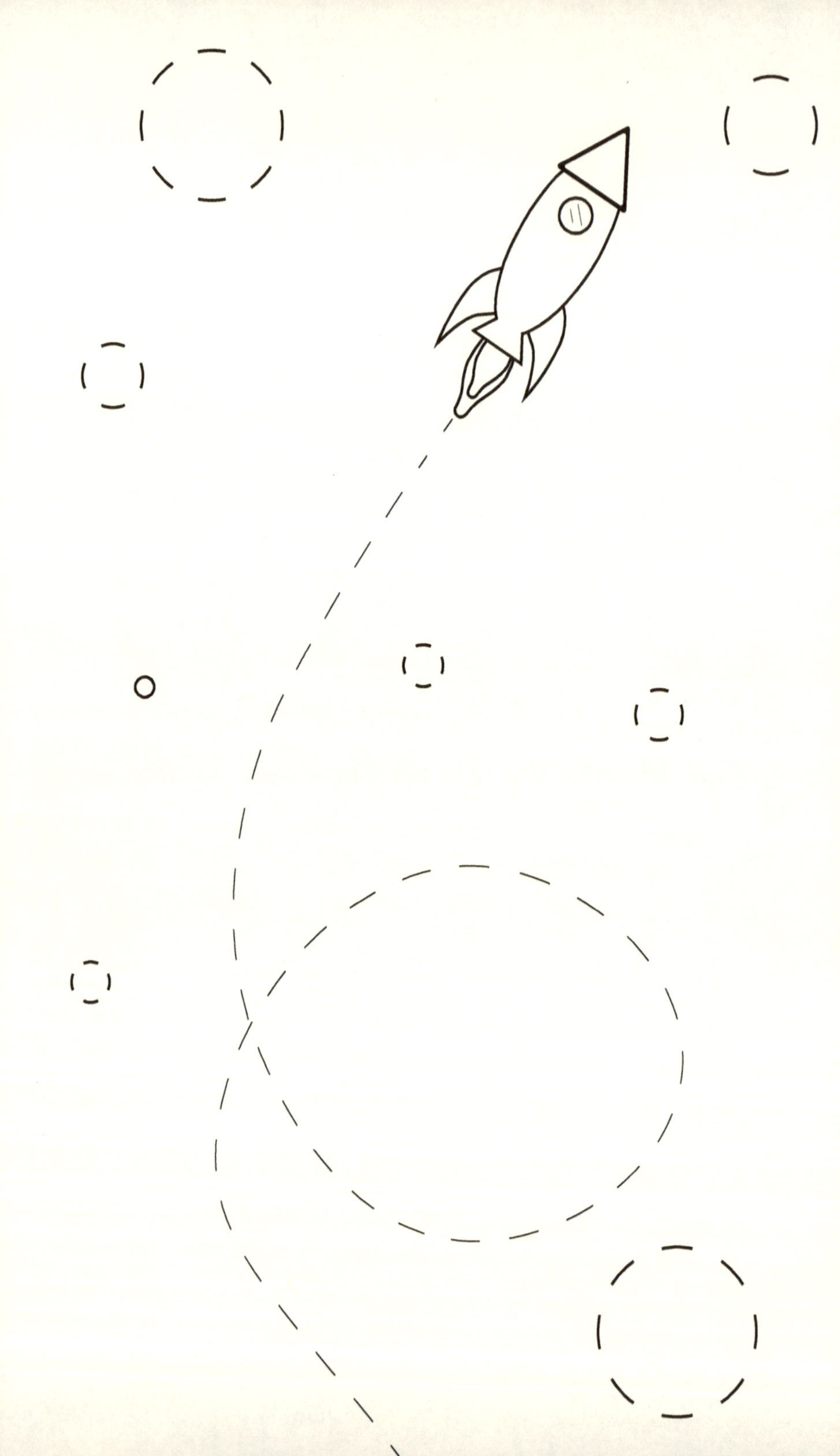

Table of Contents

INTRODUCTION

The natural world does not belong to us. Despite all of mankind's progress we are but a speck lost amidst the vastness of the universe. We often forget this. As the social pressure to constantly innovate and build increases, so too does our cumulative feeling of dominance over the world around us. As a species, particularly in the first world, we do not see ourselves as a part of nature, but rather the masters of it. We believe that world will bend to us if we only push hard enough. This idea is reenforced every time we lose another forest for another factory for another new device that can help us remember that we are the masters over the rocks we're standing on; but it really is only a feeling.

A Short Sound in the Silence deals with the idea that we can only push nature so far before it begins to push back. How in the grand scheme of things, the whole of human achievement is but a blip in the vastness of time and space. Just as soon as it arrived, it will be gone, and in the end it won't be nature that pays the consequences for humanity's actions.

This is an anthology featuring four original works, two creative pieces and two essays, all connecting back to the central theme regarding our losing battle against nature and our ultimate place in the universe.

THE SINGLE GREATEST ACHIEVEMENT OF ALL MANKIND

Jared De Roo

Seventeen Hours Before Mankind's First Jump to Light Speed

Earth had not been visible for some time now, to the lone space-craft. It sat as a single dot in a velvet universe. Though it moved quickly, its progress was invisible against the vastness of space laid out around it. A little blue plume of fire from the thrusters was the only real indication that it was moving at all. Sputtering along for months before it would be able to begin any real progress.

In the tiny ship there lived five even smaller humans. Each of them, in their own way, remembered how big everything had felt back on Earth. The ship, a colossus, towering above any monument of human achieve-ment. Themselves giants among mankind, chosen for glorious purpose. They all felt very small now. Even the blanket of stars seemed to have faded away, leaving only the jet blackness.

It was a couple weeks into the voyage when space began to close in on them. As the stars receded and the ship became enveloped in darkness, the vastness of space seemed to condense into the little microcosm of the ship, and nothing else.

Behind the treated glass panes of the little vessel, two faces stared absently out into the void. One a dark haired woman with a mousy face, the other a light haired man with a square jaw. They both stared, silently, out into the blackness. There had been a lot of talking during the first couple months of the journey. During the third month, when the tightness of space had really begun to set in it had sort of tapered off. Everyone had

---

sort of receded into themselves, they all knew what to do. Routine dominated their lives, there really just wasn't much to say anymore.

The woman stared at the console in front of her. Silently wishing for the day, if you could call it that, to end. She was ready for the routine to be shaken up a little, tomorrow the mission would really begin.

"Are you scared, Ali?"

She started, annoyed that Hans had broken the unspoken rule of silence, "I just want something to happen." She paused, unsure of whether or not she actually wanted to continue the conversation, "Are you?"

"Yah, a little."

"It should be safe."

Hans didn't respond, instead he turned back, let his eyes glaze over, and continued staring out into space.

***

Four Hours Before Mankind's First Jump to Light Speed

Jack was nervous and everyone knew it. He'd had a small mental break a few weeks ago, they'd forced him to take on extra video sessions with the mission psychologist. He was doing okay now. He mostly stayed in the lab with Hoshi, there wasn't much to do it this point. They'd check and recheck the equipment, go over the lists of samples they'd need, inspect crew biometrics, stare at the wall, and do it all again.

Over the last few days most of what they'd accomplished was making sure that they'd gotten the last of the crumbs from some sort of food Ali had brought into the lab. The lab needed to be sterile. Without gravity the little bits had floated off into seemingly every corner of the room. They'd just finished vacuuming the room for the third time, just hoping that it wouldn't wind up contaminating anything. Though Jack did think it'd be funny if they came back with samples showing signs of nutrigrain bars from other planets.

"Are we ready for tomorrow?" A thick Russian voice barked as the door to the lab opened.

"We are ready, Anna." Hoshi said absently.

Jack nodded along vigorously, "Yup, we've got everything. Just really waiting on positioning and that, you know. Ship should be where we need it in-" he paused and looked over at a timer built into the wall, "four hours. Then uh, then we can make the jump."

"Good." Anna looked around the room once more before closing the door.

As the sound of her magnetic boots faded down the hall, Jack turned to Hoshi, "She still scares me."

Hoshi was silent for a second, "She is unpleasant."

"Yeah, something like that. I just don't know what it is but something is weird about her."

"Maybe, but you would do better to worry more about the jump and less about Anna."

***

Six Minutes Before Mankind's First Jump to Light Speed

The whole crew sat huddled in front of the control panel in the cockpit of the ship. The wave of melancholy that had filled the ship for the last few months had lifted, leaving a nervous tension. Anna's fingers tapped the console in an arrhythmic beat, her grey eyes staring intently at the timer embedded in the console.

"Do you think we'll find it?"

Anna started. Everyone was silent.

"You know, find life?" Hans continued, nervous but excited.

Still no one responded. Anna had still not gotten used to Hans' nervous chatter that had plagued the crew since departure.

Hans didn't continue. Instead he too turned to the console. Five more minutes.

Jack's breathing got heavier as the countdown continued, Hoshi noted. His lack of nerves had been grating on her, but in this moment even she was beginning to feel the knot in her stomach tighten as the countdown continued. Four more minutes.

Anna's fingers tapped faster, her eyes fixated on the timer. Three more minutes.

Jack wasn't feeling great. The old feeling of panic flared up. He was paralyzed where he stood, praying it would pass when they made the jump. Two more minutes.

Ali was ready to vomit. One more minute.

***

Mankind's First Jump to Light Speed

The zeros expanded into infinity as the countdown completed, splitting reality down the middle. There was a weird moment in the nanosecond between the end of the timer and the start of the jump that lasted forever. Each moment zeroed into a tight focus and exploding beyond cognition as the universe condensed itself into the now and spread that brief frame of being into eternity. The crew themselves felt suddenly infinite. Their souls squeezed from their bodies as their conscious expanded across the universe, looking deeply into every moment at once only to bounce back and forth from every point in time and space melding together into a single bodiless mass.

And then it ended.

The weird blur of eternity closed and each crew member was left, pale faced, in their own body, feeling so small.

The silence that followed seemed endless. Everyone still in shock from the moment. The complete separation from physicality as if their bodies had moved too quickly for their souls to follow and they were just now catching up.

Jack collapsed.

Everyone, for a moment, was frozen in space, Jack hit the ground with a muted thud. Each member of the crew stood like statues until the moment caught up with them. In a second the stillness was broke. The ship shuddered as life resumed. As if someone had slammed the brakes on a fast moving car. The stillness shattered into explosive motion as the crew was thrown forward onto the console. Jack's crumpled body slammed into the glass viewport before beginning to drift listlessly around the cabin.

Anna was the first to resume motion. Her eyes darted to Jack. The others were slowly picking themselves off the floor as she disabled the magnetism in her boots and floated up to Jack. His breathing was shallow, but he seemed to be alive. She noted that one of his feet, bootless, was bent at a weird angle. Broken when the boot hadn't left the cabin floor at the same speed he did.

"Hans, help me with Jack." She ordered down.

Hans helped the two of them back to the cabin floor, with Anna back on the ground the two of them secured Jack to one of the seats.

"He's breathing. We need to do something about his foot." Anna said as she buckled Jack to the chair.

"I'll grab the medkit." Ali said quickly as she rushed out of the cabin, shaken.

"Well," Hans began, "Did we make it?" He stared out of the cabin window, the blackness had erupted into a star studded universe.

Hoshi surveyed the panel, "We made it. Everything worked. Everything but…" She paused and looked more closely.

"Everything but what?" Anna asked.

"I don't know, but look here," She motioned to the two of them, "At the very beginning of the jump, there's nothing there."

Anna pushed her aside to look for herself. There was indeed a small break in the trajectory, as if the ship had simply vanished for a second. "Probably just an error." She said.

"Probably just an error." Jack repeated.

The three of them snapped their heads around to follow the voice. Jack was sitting up, slowly beginning to unbuckle himself.

"Stay in the chair, Jack." Anna ordered, "You broke your ankle." She stared down at him, wondering if maybe he was in shock.

"Broke my ankle." Jack repeated, following Anna's inflection.

"You're in shock, Jack. Just stay still." Hans stepped towards him.

Anna almost reached out to stop him, but caught herself.

***

Ten Minutes After Mankind's First Jump to Light Speed

Ali stood still in the supply closet for a few minutes. Just breathing. Something wasn't right and she knew it. She took a deep breath. She was here for the med kit. Just grab the med kit, she told herself. She had seen something during the jump. A brief moment, a split second. Somewhere between the jump and infinity, that second of forever before they hit light speed something had slipped onto the ship. She remembered that as her soul flowed out her eyes in the brief in-between there was a wisp of black tendrils snaking across the exterior of the ship. She could've sworn she saw it swirling inside of Jack before she returned to her own body. The med kit.

"Ali." Anna's voice cracked through her earpiece, "Return to the bridge. We do not need the med kid. Return to the bridge. We're going home."

Ali froze. Anna may not have been the most polished person, but her voice seemed to have the quality of someone just learning to speak a new language.

"Ali, we're going home."

She tapped the button on her transmitter, "I-I'm on my way back." A wave of dread washed over her as she made her return to the bridge.

***

Twenty Five Minutes After Mankind's First Jump to Light Speed

"Are we authorized to return without samples?" Ali asked nervously.

"We are authorized to return without samples." Hans stared directly at her, a sickly sort of smile fixed on his lips.

This wasn't right. None of this was right. Ali tried to suppress her panic. She had checked through the instrument board to find nothing, except a minor blip in the readings, out of place. There was no reason to head back, not that she could think of at least. "Um, Anna, w-why are we going back? The ship's reading everything fine."

"Orders." Anna smiled.

"We…we can't receive transmissions after the jump, Anna." Ali moved to stand out of her seat. Before she could get to her feet she felt a hand on her shoulder. Hans weighed down on her, softly but firmly.

"We need to get Jack home, Ali." Hans motioned somberly towards Jack.

"We need to get me home, Ali." Jack stepped forward, his ankle making a hideous crack under his shifting weight.

"Hans…Jack…"Ali's apprehension turned to dread, "We have orders, we need to collect the samples."

Anna moved closer, "There is not time. We need to get home soon."

"But Anna, the ship's fine, Jack…Jack will be fine…we have provisions. We're prepared for things like this." Ali's voice cracked as the tone of the room darkened.

"That's an order, Ali." Anna's voice sharpened.

"Okay." Ali sat silently for a second. Something in the pit of her stomach was beginning to clench. "Hans?"

Hans stared, unmoving.

"Hans, I need your help to reset the jump drive. I can't do this alone."

Hans hesitated, "Are you certain?"

Ali was taken aback, "What do you mean? You have the other key, I can't access the controls without it. We just did this."

Anna stepped up, "Take his key, you need to do this without him."

"I don't understand is something wrong?" Ali's heart sank.

"Ali, please just take us home." Hoshi's voice cracked.

"I…"Ali began to choke up, she took a pause, swallowed, and shakily continued, "I don't know what's happening right now."

Jack lurched forward, "Ali, are you okay?" His ankle was beginning to soak in red.

Hans spent an awkward moment searching himself for the key, he found it hung around his neck. "Here's my key."

"Just…Just put it in the keyhole there," She pointed to the other side of the panel, "We'll turn them at the same time…like before."

Hans fumbled with his key, it took them a couple tries to sync up their key turns, even though they'd done this hundreds of times in training. Ali felt a bead of sweat forming on her forehead. "Why are we going home, Anna?"

Anna stared at her for a moment, "We're running low on food."

"We just took stock before the jump though, we have enough for at least another year."

Anna's face tightened. "I am running low on food." She stared pointedly at Ali. "Take us home. Now."

Ali froze. Four pairs of eyes glared down at her. For a moment no one spoke, Ali began to feel as if the world was growing around her and she was, all of a sudden, very small.

"Now." Anna growled, placing a threatening hand on her shoulder.

Ali hesitated at the controls for a moment, contemplating the consequences of what she was about to do. Finally, with half a strangled sob, she gritted her teeth, and began setting up the sequence. "I need your fingerprint, Anna." She whispered as she shakily completed the operation.

Anna smiled, removed her hand from Ali's shoulder, and authenticated the launch sequence. Ali felt her heart sink as the autopilot locked.

The world didn't bend around them this time. Rather it skipped in a sickening lurch as the ship began to jettison fuel reserves, blasting forward at full power with what was left in the tanks. A muted sob escaped Ali.

"Ali, why is the ship not jumping." Anna's voice carried a tinge of panic.

Ali stayed silent.

Anna leapt forward, lifted her from her seat, and in a single motion threw her against console. "What did you do?" She barked.

Ali's eyes flinched to the quickly emptying fuel gauge.

Hoshi jumped to the controls, but paused before touching them, hands prepared but frozen, as if trying to remember how they worked. "Fix it, Ali!" She finally screamed.

Ali set her jaw, "I can't."

Four pairs of eyes locked on her. "Take us home, Ali." They said in unison.

Ali closed her eyes, "I won't." She whispered.

***

Two Thousand Years After Mankind's First Jump to Light Speed

The little ship, almost invisible against the black felt canvas behind it, hurtled along through the universe. Momentum fueling its eternal voyage. The rockets had died out long ago. Now the speck was free to sail along the infinite expanse without interruption. Millions of miles past and trillions of miles to go. The ship was in no hurry and the universe would be there a while yet, so the little craft sailed on.

WHEN THE GIRL FELL

Rose Watson

"Nature's creative power is far beyond man's instinct of destruction."
–Jules Verne

The girl didn't know when the wing hit her. One moment she was darting across a bridge, the familiar thrum of the metal support ropes echoing in her shins, and the next… She was flying. For half a second she hung, frozen and suspended in the air, a true flying fish. And then the ringing in her head came into focus. A warm feeling coated her temple and then her cheek and the wind began to push at her clothes and limbs. She had a moment to turn toward the sea, sparkling below.

She plummeted.

***

"Do you taste it, sister?" the raw edge of the old man's voice had broken the calm of the early morning meditation. An uncomfortable murmur rumbled through the congregation. The captain had been silent for thirteen months. He had been in the middle of a sermon when the tide drew out. They said that the sea took his voice because she loved the way it sounded. No one knew if she'd ever give it back.

"Do you taste it?" he said again, looking to the woman sitting to his right. The congregation had gotten used to going through the meditations and services with a mute leader, and no one had taken on more service than Lorelei, a tired twenty something who had found purpose in the small, fervent community of the Church of Our Tidal Mother. She was staring, eyes wide, at her captain.

"I don't…"

"Do you taste it girl! The air is flowing with salt this day. A great wave is coming for our city. We will see the way that the mother protects her children." The old man, stood suddenly and strode through the circle of faithful. They parted in stunned silence, hanging on the words of the old man. He hadn't moved this easily since before the rot. The staff he had relied on for the past four years was abandoned at his seat, "Yes my friends! Can you taste it? This is the dawn of a blessed day. We must welcome it!"

He had reached the solid double doors of the chapel. They were big and sturdy, made of the recycled side paneling of a retired naval ship. The captain grabbed the handles of the doors and pulled, dragging them open in one motion. He stood, his full body haloed with light from the sun breeching over the horizon of the sea. Lorelei had stumbled after him, desperate to help her guru, but stopped at seeing his eyes streaming with tears. They flowed down his face, and he made no move to wipe them away.

"Sister," his voice had hushed so only Lorelei could hear him, "I am called. I leave my ship to you." The old man died.

***

The girl had been born decades after the city drowned. She'd heard stories of the dry city, how there was pavement and sidewalks and most people owned dogs or cats. She had seen old photos of dry boats that used to fill the streets from morning to night; Miss Angela, the old lady who she paged to quite often, had called them cars. Miss Angela told her once that you couldn't even see the ocean from the street when she was a girl. The levees were too high. She and her friends would go on picnics on the crown of the levee and joke about how the world would end. Miss Angela would get very quiet after saying things like this. The girl found it odd, because the world hadn't ended after all. But she didn't tell Miss Angela that.

Five million people died after the first flooding. Another four and a half died after the second rupture. But the real killer was the skin rot. Something in the sea reacted to the sealant on the streets and a toxic element was formed. It leeched into the bodies of refugees. It saturated the relief food and the blankets that were constantly damp and musty. Curing it was easy: stay dry. But that wasn't as simple as it sounded. Eventually, Neheti Crane developed a sort of cure, and like a crusading hero, proclaimed the safety of the people bellow while selling each injection at a price. Ten million more people rotted away while the city began to rebuild.

Cults began to crop up begging forgiveness and protection from the sea. Some begged help from the Virgin Mary, others Poseidon, merfolk, Li Ban, Lir, Mazu, Samundra, Yemoja, and countless others. New prophets claimed to be able to heal the skin rot. Some just wanted to create new families when all others were lost. The girl's parents didn't believe in much of anything anymore. They used to, but there is only so much you can hold onto. The girl just liked the songs that she could hear from the small chapels built on the lower deck where she lived.

"You absolute imbecile!" Dr. Reiksac been waiting for him to land on the wide balcony that jutted out from the side of the laboratory floor. He could see through the broad windows of the lab that all her assistants and researchers were gone.

"This was not my fault." The man stripped off his gloves and threw them on the ground.

"Like hell this wasn't your fault! What kind of egotist flies unfinished tech in between decks?"

"I had control," his voice came out clearer as he took off the helmet, "You told me to put the wing-suit through its paces; I did. You were the one that designed the safety protocols to freeze out the goddamn pilot!"

"You should never have flown in between bridges and promenades. The programming had an error; that's what this experiment was for! Finding problems. Not endangering civilians before we're even on the market!" In anger, Dr. Reiksac threw a clipboard to the ground, splaying papers across the sleek, black floor of the lab.

"I wouldn't have if your tech had worked right!" There were a few moments of silence. Barron Holiday could see Dr. Reiksac was seething as she glared at him. Her fists had gone as white as her lab coat from being clenched. He was sweating and breathing hard. He broke the staring contest to stumble to a carafe of cold water. Holiday poured himself a shaky glass and downed it, falling into a chair by the counter.

"Did you see what happened to her?" Dr. Reiksac's voice had lost its hot fury and had gone ice cold.

"She fell."

"No shit, Holiday." the pilot wiped a hand down his face.

"She popped out of nowhere. The proximity alarm went off; it froze me out. I couldn't pull up or retract the wings. I tried to roll, but I didn't have time." Dr. Reiksac took a deep breath and pushed her shiny black hair back from her face. She stepped to the counter and rested her knuckles on the cool surface.

"She was young too. We are going to be crucified for this one. At least shewasn't anyone's daughter." Holiday stared at her as she pushed off the counter and pulled up a command screen, deftly opening several message windows to send to various assistants and PR personnel.

"What do you mean she wasn't anyone's daughter, of course she was!" he poured himself another glass. Dr. Reiksac didn't turn around.

"Yes, but not to anyone important."

***

The girl got the page job when she turned ten. She had lived most of her life dashing around the lower decks and, like any child born in the drowned city, had natural sea legs. She could run across a choppy inter-section with an open jug of water without spilling a drop. She'd taken the lid off of one just to see if she could. While paging didn't pay well, it was something to contribute to their families. The girl's mother, Tala, spent a week's wages on good sturdy boots for her and dubbed the girl her, "little flying fish". Most people in the lower decks would call after her as she dart-ed up the creaking staircases and whipped around corners.

****

Lorelei had been wandering the city. She hadn't known what to do after the captain's passing. The burden of the congregation seemed to choke her mind. She had managed to catch the captain's body before he fell, but he was gone. The eyes of the church... her church gazed up, searching for direction. She had barely been able to stumble over an excuse before fleeing. The sun had been in her eyes as she cried silently through the streets of the drowned city.

She walked down a shady promenade, stepping out into the light in the square with open water in the middle. The sun felt good on her tired body and she tilted her head up to feel it. The light pricked at her puffy eyelids.

A scream struck Lorelei out of her trance. She started, opening her eyes to see a small figure hit the water hard. There was a woman on a lower bridge pointing and shouting at the place the figure had fallen.

She kicked off her old boots and dove for the cold, dark water.

***

"They killed my baby! They killed her and want to give me shut-up money! They won't even give me her body! I want you buzzards out of my house! I want you gone!" Tala wailed to the crowd outside their small home. The neighbors had gathered when they saw black suits waiting outside the mourning mother's home. Black suits meant trouble or money most times, both of which were the best kind of gossip. The girl's father was crushed by the news. Her mother was enraged. She'd lost one daughter to the rot and a son to the cults. The girl was her last child. Her grief echoed through the lower deck and caught flame. The black suits shuffled awkwardly away back to their roost.

The young people began to organize and speechify. The elders hung black banners and sang old songs of rebellion. The bridges to the upper decks were torn down by crowds of angry hands.

***

An emergency crew pushed their way through the crowd. There were onlookers from upper levels, but the crowd that gathered on the walkway surrounding where she fell was thick. There were the voyeurs who always showed up with tragedy and the concerned citizens and wide-eyed children. The dive crew was met with a young woman kneeling on the boardwalk, her blue dress soaked and clinging to her body, her wide eyes darted franticly, and her chest heaving. She was clutching the small girl in her arms; blood from the girl's temple was staining the fabric at her breast. The crew took the girl; the woman resisted for a moment, then released her burden.

"I taste it, Captain. I taste it." she had been whispering to herself. Most likely shock, the emergency team reported. After the girl had been taken Lorelei looked at the responder who had the girl.

"She's important. Be careful with her."

The girl was already dead.

***

There were a few still nights after she fell. The lower decks were grieving. The lantern boats they lit on the calm night water made their memorial vigil a haunting view to the upper decks. The well-to-do had a hard time sleeping because of the tension in the air. The light coming from below bounced up the slick granite walls and created an undying sunset they couldn't avoid, except to pull all the curtains closed and be in unnatural darkness. They were left to listen to the hymns and ululations that echoed to their nests. The noise was worse in the dark. Fish weren't supposed to sing.

***

The water was cold and deep and darker than it seemed it should have been. Lorelei could see the small figure of the girl just feet below her. She strained to swim faster while her breath began to feel small and hard in her throat. The girl was sinking too fast.

But then she stopped sinking.

She was suspended in the water, almost as if a thread had been pulled from her narrow chest reaching up from the depths toward the surface. Lorelei started, a burst of bubbles coming from her mouth. She tried to swim farther to grab her but was also suspended, unable to move. The water began to warm and swirl around the pair. The pressure from Lorelei's lungs began to ease and she felt an impossible new breath in her chest. The girl began to glow, a soft blue-green light emanated from her chest. She opened her eyes, now glowing the same blue-green light, and spoke something incomprehensible to the woman in the water. Lorelei could only stare transfixed.

The warm current swirled and intertwined around the couple, cradling them. The light seemed to sooth and they drifted up and up toward the surface. Lorelei could almost hear singing in the water like a voice she knew once, but faint and far away. It felt like being home.

Then the light disappeared and the sea went cold and her lungs were burning and the girl was drifting once more. Lorelei grabbed the girl and pushed for the surface.

***

Nehiti Crane leaned on the railing of his penthouse balcony looking at the destruction below. He had a glass of wine swirling in his palm and a serious look on his face. Dr. Reiksac and Barron Holiday stared coolly across the space at each other. They'd been asked to have an audience with Crane, the most imposing man in the city. A wailing scream echoed over the distant noise, and Crane took a sip of a vintage. It was a bottle from before the city drowned, the taste was different somehow, less salty. He ran a dark hand over his shaven head.

"Mr. Crane, sir?" Holiday's voice was thinner than normal with a thread of fear weaving through it.

"A fine mess you two have made of my city," His voice was deep and had almost a sing-song cadence, "I do not blame you though." Holiday opened his mouth to speak, but Nehiti continued, "This was in the works far before the girl. A city needs to purge every so often. They will fight themselves out, and the chum will wash out to sea. A great catharsis of man. And we are lucky enough to have our safe perch up here, to witness the event."

He paused looking over the vista. There were fires, bridges burned and gasoline fires floating on the high tides. Riot police were cruising in boats and sectioning off different waterways. Neighborhoods had been sprayed with riot gas. Skin rot injections had already been embargoed. Twenty five people had succumbed in the last four days.

"Isn't it extraordinary, the nature of man?"

WOLVES OF THE FOREST

Jared De Roo

> I found myself astray in a dark wood
> where the straight road had been lost sight of.
> How hard it is to say what it was like
> in the thick of thickets, in a wood so dense
> and gnarled
> the very thought of it renews my panic.
> – Dante's Inferno, Cato 1

The machine moves forever forward. There is a prevailing idea that the systematic destruction of the environment will never find its way back to us. Mankind has marched onward through history abusing the world around them in order to build themselves up. It is this anthropocentric arrogance that we believe sets us apart from the natural world, when in reality we are not quite the masters of it that we think. This arrogance towards the natural world, and its consequences are shown throughout the first season of the Netflix Original, Stranger Things. Nature is not a silent victim of industry. We can only push so far before we find ourselves helpless against what we have unleashed.

The show takes place in the early 1980s when a young Will Byers disappeared from the sleepy town of Hawkins, Indiana. His disappearance started a series of strange events. It all begins in the forest. Will was riding home from playing Dungeons & Dragons with his friends when, passing through the forest they nicknamed Mirkwood, he is run off the road by a shadowy creature. His bike is left abandoned in the murky forest as Will makes the rest of his escape home on foot. The creature chases him, confronts him in the shed behind his house, and pulls him into what they call the "Upside Down." The Upside Down is a dark mirror of reality. It crawls with organic matter and thick mucus. The sky is black, the air cold, but the world itself is a reflection of ours. This abduction kicks off a series of events, prompting a city-wide search for Will. His close friends: Mike, Dustin, and Lucas, set off on their own adventure to find their missing friend (Duffer, Chapter One: The Vanishing of Will Byers).

The search for Will begins in the forest. His bicycle is found, discarded, in Mirkwood. As a result, the search parties are heavily focused on the surrounding wooded areas. This is the beginning of man's interaction with nature in the series; adventuring in to find what was taken. Will's friends, in particular, are affected by the forest. It is a place where they are forced to take part in a world much bigger than themselves. They are no longer thirteen year olds playing D&D in their basements. Rather, they are the pieces on the quest run by a higher power. Once they enter the forest in their search for Will, they leave childhood behind, dealing with the responsibility forced on them. Nature has taken charge as the Dungeon Master in this new game. In her two part work, From Sacred Grove to Dark Wood to Re-enchanted Forest, Joy Greenburg talks about the role of the forest through several different cultures and time periods. Throughout history, and through many different cultures and mythologies, the forest symbolized initiation. "The forest has always been a place of initiation, for there the demonic presences, the ancestral spirits, and the forces of nature reveal themselves" (Greenburg, 4). The demonic presence and forces of nature from the Upside Down in Stranger Things mirrors this idea of initiation in the forest that Greenburg brings up. The children venture into the woods hoping to find their friend, but there is much more waiting for them. This is their rite of passage into a world much larger than themselves. Their first real challenge comes with the discovery of Eleven in Mirkwood.

Eleven herself is a force of nature that the government scientists are trying to control. She is a child, around the same age as Will, who was born with telekinetic abilities as a result of her mother being involved in government funded MK Ultra experimentation (Duffer, Chapter Six: The Monster). The laboratory where they kept her before her escape sat outside of the little town of Hawkins, right next to Mirkwood. It was there where she was found by Mike, Dustin, and Lucas. She sits in an in-be-tween, connecting the raw forces of nature to the world of man. It was because the scientists attempted to use her supernatural ability that the portal to the Upside Down opened in the first place, as she alone held that connection with the otherworld. Eleven is a conduit to the natural world, an outsider with powers that not only set her apart from the human race, but gives the government a reason to commodify her. As a result of their attitude towards nature, Eleven only mattered to them as far as they could use her and her abilities to manipulate the world around them. It is during their attempt to weaponize her when they accidentally open the gate to the Upside Down in their very own laboratory. It is the escape into the wil-derness that allows Eleven to become herself, free from the confinement of the laboratory.

Eleven's connection with nature comes from her ability to not only manipulate the physical world around her, but also the connection she has with the Upside Down. She is both in the world as a member of the human race, but also has control of certain aspects of nature that set her as an in-between. Eleven is originally found in forest by the boys. In this same forest Nancy and Jonathan found the portal to the Upside Down. By placing these pieces in the forest the show is able to show that they repre-sent nature in its most primal form. In Greenburg's work she talks about how Thoreau's vision of the forest supports this. "For Thoreau, the forest was clearly a place where he believed he could touch primordial elements raw, pure, and sacred" (Greenburg, 11). Eleven's connection with nature is made more significant because she was found in the forest (Duffer, Chap-ter One: The Vanishing of Will Byers). The show builds on this idea by naming the forest Mirkwood, connecting it to the forest in The Lord of the Rings and The Hobbit. In these books the forest is described as a dark and foreboding place, filled with unseen evil. In The Hobbit, Tolkien describes the forest, "By the afternoon they had reached the eves of Mirkwood, and were resting almost beneath the great overhanging boughs of its outer trees. Their trunks were huge and gnarled, their branches twisted, their leaves were dark and long" (Tolkien, 134). Eleven is a light in the darkness, the forest that houses the creature from the Upside Down also delivers the one who will ultimately vanquish it.

Nature is a powerful force throughout the series and it takes many forms, from the symbolism in the trees, to the supernatural and unexplainable. Nature is manifested through these otherworldly occurrences as a force that humanity both unleashed and is powerless to stop. This problem in the series comes from man's belief that nature is unquestionably theirs to use. Shepard, in his work "Ecology and Man" talks about the anthropocentrism that caused the ecological crisis in the first place. "Now we find ourselves in a deteriorating environment which breeds aggressiveness and hostility toward ourselves and our world" (Shepard, 63). Stranger Things shows a much more visceral example of this, with the uncaring scientists ultimately being brutally killed by what they released. This is similar to the way the destruction of the environment for the sake of industry in today's world creates the same kind of vengeance from nature, granted on a longer timeline with less demonic creatures. Shepard talks about man's refusal to recognize their own place in nature, seeing themselves as above it, believing its very existence is for their own benefit, "The rejection of animality is a rejection of nature as a whole" (Shepard, 66). By not wanting to admit that we are animals, and a part of nature, we are destroying not only our world, but ourselves.

It is interesting to note that while the government agents and scientists show a clear desire to master nature, they are never seen entering it. Almost every other character in the series is at some point or another found traveling, running, or searching through the forest. But those who are so keen about mastering it are never once seen in it. Stranger Things uses the forest to house the unknown. It calls back to a more archaic view of the wilderness. In his work "The Trouble with Wilderness; or, Getting Back to the Wrong Nature," William Cronon talks not only about the pre-industrial view of the forest that Stranger Things calls back to, but also the false idea of wilderness that humanity has fabricated, "Wilderness, in short, was a place to which one came only against one's will, and always in fear and trembling…in its raw state, it had little or nothing to offer civilized men and women" (Cronon, 103). According to Cronon the idea that the wilderness is something to enter on a whim is a relatively new one. Before the romantics turned it into a sacred wonderland the forest was feared. It was a matter of power, before we were able to sanitize the forest, it was a foreboding place fraught with danger. As the danger and mystery subsided this fear of death and the unknown faded with it. In Stranger Things the fact that those responsible for releasing the creature into the forest are the only ones who never set foot in it calls back to this power imbalance.

By staying removed from nature, the scientists maintained their separation from it. This separation allowed them to stay, in their minds, above the natural world. Cronon builds on this idea saying, "The wilderness is not quite what it seems. Far from being the one place on earth that stands apart from humanity, it is quite profoundly a human creation" (Cronon, 102). They had to further this idea of "the wilderness" to allow themselves to commit the crimes against nature that they did. By solidifying the wilderness as a separate entity there for man's use they could remove the ethical issue of actually abusing it for their own gain.

From an ecological perspective Stranger Things is a story about man's failure to master nature. By abusing Eleven's abilities they opened a portal that they were unable to comprehend or control (Duffer, Chapter Six: The Monster). Their fear of the creature they had unleashed connects to their absence from the forest throughout the show. The forest was not welcoming to them because they had lost control over it. Cronon describes the feeling of locking eyes with an animal as follows, "Remember the feelings of such moments, and you will know as well as I do that you were in the presence of something irreducibly nonhuman, something profoundly other than yourself" (Cronon, 103). This sensation of the profoundly other is extremely pronounced throughout the show. It creates a side to nature that is so fully alien that suddenly the places that we went to escape civilization revert back, for a moment, to the savage unknown of years past.

There is no salvation for the scientists who attempted to conquer nature. Rather, it was only after each of them had been killed, either by the monster or Eleven, that any resolution was reached in the show. (Duffer, Chapter Eight: The Upside Down). Ultimately, it was Eleven that vanquished the monster. She sits in the middle between mankind and nature, not fully in either world, but able to work between them. By removing the distinction between the two worlds, Eleven is as an equalizer, ridding both worlds of its demons. The scientists worked to create walls between mankind and nature, setting up a world where they were undeniably the masters. The fact that it was their attempt to commodify Eleven that was ultimately their downfall speaks to the hubris of this anthropocentric world view.

Man's determination to advance themselves at the expense of nature involves the systematic destruction and reformation of the environment. In order to push themselves forward they not only use and destroy nature but also reshape it to fit their needs. In the case of Eleven, the group of scientists broke her down before building her back in a way that was beneficial for them. In Greenwood's essay she talks about Tolkien's Fangorn and it being ravaged by Saruman's henchmen.

> In depicting this devastated forest, Tolkien apparently envisioned a revolt by environmental activists–in this case the Ents of Fangorn Forest–who at one point became so enraged by the desolation of their arboreal homeland that they fought back.
> (Greenwood, 15)

This is, in essence, what happened in Stranger Things. Man pushed too hard and nature revolted. It can be argued too that the monster that they released was not evil in and of itself, rather just a creature whose home had been disturbed by mankind. Much like the Ents in Lord of the Rings, the creatures in it are a neutral force. Letting the monster loose in our reality could be likened to letting a wolf loose in a chicken pen, the guilt for the dead chickens lays not with the wolf, but with whoever let it in.

The narrative of man verses nature has been done in many different ways over the years and it will continue to for many more. The ecological significance of Stranger Things speaks to the futility of man's constant battle for mastery over nature. It highlights how we have framed our dominion over the earth, how while we may be destroying the world in the end we are working more towards exterminating ourselves for short term gain. To quote Neil deGrasse Tyson, "Earth will survive this. People say

'Save the earth.' No, don't worry about earth. Earth'll be here long after we render ourselves extinct" (Tyson, 1:10-1:17). In the end, nature will always win.

Works Cited

Alighieri, Dante, and Mark Musa. Inferno. Penguin Books, 1984. Print.
Baillie, De Souza Christie, and J. R. R. Tolkien. The Hobbit. Alt house Press, 1989. Print.

Cronon, William. "The Trouble with Wilderness; or, Getting Back to the Wrong Nature." Ecocriticism: The Essential Reader. Ed. Ken Hilt ner. New York: Routledge, 2015. 102-119. Print.

Duffer, Matt and Ross, creators. Stranger Things, Written and Directed by the Duffer Brothers, Netflix, 2016.

Greenberg, Joy H. "From Sacred Grove to Dark Wood to Re-Enchanted Forest (Part II): The Evolution of Arborphilia as Neo-Romantic Environmental Ethics." Journal for the Study of Religion, Nature & Culture, vol. 9, no. 4, Oct. 2015, pp. 414-447. EBSCOhost, doi: 10.1558/jsrnc.v9i4.28906.

Shepard, Paul. "Ecology and Man: A Viewpoint." Ecocriticism: The Essential Reader. Ed. Ken Hiltner. New York: Routledge, 2015. 62-69. Print.

Wei, Will. "Neil deGrasse Tyson: Don't Worry, Earth Will Survive Climate Change - We Won't." Business Insider, Business Insider, 1 May 2014, www.businessinsider.com/neil-degrasse-tyson-climate-change-greenhouse-gas-2014-4.

THE NATURE DICHOTOMY IN FRANKENSTEIN: THE MONSTER

Savannah McClellan

Western civilization has disassociated itself from nature; as if there is such a thing as a person without nature or vice versa. As a culture, those that reside in the United States grow up with a Christian doctrine. There are many religious groups with differing views, but one story that dominates is that of Adam and Eve. In Genesis, it is written that "God blessed them, and God said unto them, be fruitful, and multiply, and replenish the earth, and subdue it: and have dominion over the fish of the sea, and over the fowl of the air, and over every living thing that moveth upon the earth" (Genesis 1:28 KJV). This set forth the idea that dominion is the way we should interact with nature. This story is the beginning of what has become a complete lack of association and understanding of what nature is and why humans are included in that term. Humans and nature are inextricable and the idea that they are and should be separate, where humans dominate nature, has led to the outcome of mutual destruction.

The novel Frankenstein, by Mary Shelley, exhibits a human using his dominion over nature to create nature of his own. This creation is a symbol of the nature/human divide. A human, doctor Frankenstein, dominates nature by using natural resources and human body parts to form something of his own imagining. In result, the thing he creates is monstrous. This monstrosity is not in the comingling of nature and humanity, because this is the natural state, it is in the creation process of this formation. Shelley creates a physical representation of the conflict between humans and nature. The monster is more obviously from nature than that of a human, because he was created with nature elements and not born of a person's body. And yet, he is created by the hands of Frankenstein. This combination allows nature to have the conscience of humanity and speak on the injustice done to it.

The story of Frankenstein is a distress call to see the link between humanity and nature as something you should care about, not abhor. The monster is seen as outside of nature; unnatural. This is the wrong assumption. The monster is both from nature and made by man. He has thoughts, feelings, and the same survival instinct of any living thing. After being abandoned at birth, the monster seeks out Frankenstein and like a child, reaches out for his creator to love and nurture him. In response, Frankenstein says, "His jaws opened, and he muttered some inarticulate sounds, while a grin wrinkled his cheeks… one hand was stretched out, seemingly to detain me" (Shelley 36). The monster wanted his creator to nurture him and found that his creator did not want him from the start. Barbara Kingsolver, in her essay "High Tide in Tucson" gave herself this reminder, "Let me never forget to distinguish want from need. Let me be a good animal today" (1077). In its essence, this quote is to remind us that we are all animals, but as humans, we must keep our wants in check. The monster's combination of human and nature allows him to speak to this animal connection. He was created to satisfy Frankenstein's want for experimental creation, but the monster was given no avenue to satisfy his need of survival.

The monster is nature and human. This superficially created connection is a scream of horror that humans see themselves as separate from nature, when nature is humanity. The monster in Frankenstein not only represents the nature/human divide, but also the destruction when humans attempt to dominate and control elements of nature. His existence as both human and nature is what makes him so abhorrent in the story and results in his isolation. The monster is rejected by his creator and when he reads Paradise Lost, he realizes that the isolation imposed on him by his creator is not the case for Adam. The monster says, "He had come forth from the hands of God a perfect creature, happy and prosperous, guarded by the especial care of his Creator" (90). Victor Frankenstein abandoned his creation. This isolation and otherness is then what led to his murderous rampage. When nature is abused and defined as other than human, it becomes dangerous to humans. In the story, the monster claims revenge, but in nature it is survival. Nature will fight for its right to exist and we cannot exist without it.

Humanity either wants to fight nature or preserve nature, but this fails to acknowledge that any act involving nature also involves humans. When nature and humanity operate together organically, they function sustainably. For simplicity's sake, let us call this term the human natural. The answer is to reconcile nature with humanity and come to the human natural. When we as human beings see ourselves as nature, we will cease trying to control what is already a part of us. Gary Snyder develops this idea and adds to it the idea of the Commons. He writes that, "We need to make a world-scale 'Natural Contract' with the oceans, the air, the birds in the sky. The challenge is to bring the whole world of 'common pool resources' into the mind of the Commons" (75). As humans, we have abused nature to the point that the Tragedy of the Commons is applicable to much more than pastures where the cows are fed. We have depleted nature and the answer is not preservation, but sustainable coexistence.

Victor Frankenstein perpetuates this violation of nature when he aspires to be a scientist in order to better understand and control nature. He attends a lecture where professor M. Waldman talks about the wonders that a scientist can perform. He says, "They have acquired new and almost unlimited powers; they can command the thunders of heaven, mimic the earthquake, and even mock the invisible world with its own shadows" (29). Victor Frankenstein sees nature for its utility. First, Frankenstein uses nature as sublime regeneration. He notes many moments in the story when he was rejuvenated by nature, sometimes brought back from the brink of despair. At one moment, Frankenstein confesses that, "When happy, inanimate nature had the power of bestowing on me the most delightful sensations. A serene sky and verdant fields filled me with ecstasy" (Shelley 45). The physical appearance and presence of nature is important to Frankenstein's being. He values nature for its beauty.

The second way in which Frankenstein sees nature for its utility is by what he can physically create with it and use it for. He desires in the beginning to create a being dependent upon and worshipful of him. He takes on a god role of creation. He thinks; "A new species would bless me as its creator and source; many happy and excellent natures would owe their being to me. No father could claim the gratitude of his child so completely as I should deserve their's" (33). Frankenstein's conviction that he could utilize nature for his own means was his downfall. The monster was rejected by his creator because of his perceived grotesque combination of human and nature. This put the monster firmly into the category of other. The monster was created by man, taught to see the world as a man, but rejected by all men as other. It is useful to see the monster as the other because he does not exist in a world of nature and humanity as one, but a dichotomy where he cannot exist. He cannot exist in this world because people see through the eyes of the dichotomy, which is not tolerant of a middle ground. Nature in its current state is set apart from humanity, which is why Frankenstein's monster becomes dangerous and sinister. If the divide dissolved naturally, the resulting creation would be harmonious and thriving; the human natural would not result in a monster.

As long as Frankenstein's monster is considered as the other, his existence in the nature/humanity dichotomy is a problem. As ecocritic Timothy Mortan notes in his essay "Frankenstein and Ecocriticism", "If ecological criticism is about critiquing and transcending anthropocentrism, it needs to get past this mode, the mode in which there is construction, and something that is constructed, and a sharp difference between human beings and everything else" (Morton 146). When Frankenstein created the monster, he separated himself from the monster's actions. Frankenstein did not feel responsible for his creation until after the monster retaliated. Through creation Frankenstein extended his nature to the monster. If our origin story is reevaluated not as one of domination, but of equal coexistence, the human natural would dissolve the category of other. William Cronon, in his work "The Trouble with Wilderness; or, Getting Back to the Wrong Nature," states that "For many Americans wilderness stands as the last remaining place where civilization, that all too human disease, has not fully infected the earth. It is an island in the polluted sea of urban-industrial modernity," he continues on to say that is where we can escape (102). But, escape from what? The human natural means that there is no escape, only dealing with the internal problems of our world.

All things are linked. Plants, animals, people, are all a part of the same thing. The roots of the belief that division between these things is not only right, but necessary, can be traced back to the Christian origin story as previously noted. The western world has long been conceived on the story of Adam and Eve, resulting in the misconception that dominion is God's will. Lynn White Jr. wrote "The Historical Roots of Our Ecological Crisis" and follows this thread as he relates Christianity's history of destroying pagan animism. He writes that, "Christianity made it possible to exploit nature in a mood of indifference to the feelings of natural objects" (White 43). Frankenstein thought he had the right to use nature for its utility and create a being of his own imagining. The western world promotes this behavior as rightful progress. Humans continue to experiment on nature in order to create a better surrounding for themselves, without regard to the nature they are exploiting. In the dichotomy, it makes sense that nature is something that can be utilized without consequence for humans. They are separate and what happens to one does not correlate with what happens to the other. However, because the dichotomy is a flawed image of our existence, it misconstrues the following consequences as isolated from human acts.

Christian axioms commodify nature. This is not an intentional act, yet the dichotomy remains intact. In Frankenstein, the monster reproaches Frankenstein for his behavior. He says, "You, my creator, detest and spurn me, thy creature, to whom thou art bound by ties only dissoluble by the annihilation of one of us. You purpose to kill me. How dare you sport thus with life?" (Shelley 68). Frankenstein did not see the probable consequences of his actions because what he planned to create was not human. He saw an opportunity to commodify nature to meet his ends and quickly took it. It was not until the monster killed Frankenstein's loved ones in revenge that Frankenstein felt responsible for him. He desired the destruction of what he had so easily created without considering the changed state of the monster. The monster was no longer pieces of human and animal on an operation table. He was not just meat that could be cleaved again. It is this consideration of consequence that is overlooked in nature. In an ending comment, Lynn White writes, "We shall continue to have a worsening ecologic crisis until we reject the Christian axiom that nature has no reason for existence save to serve man" (White 46). We have urbanized to the point that there is no "wilderness" to escape to. If we cannot see the human natural when we look in the mirror, we will destroy ourselves.

In scary movies, when the inanimate thing moves, the kids scream "It…It's ALIVE!" and they run. When something is classified as alive, it has more worth. When it has a conscience, we say it has rights. But we fail to realize that we are the voice of nature and in result any right we have must also be given to nature. Frankenstein created the monster and he has worth and rights. The monster attempts to reason with Frankenstein,

> 'You are in the wrong,' replied the fiend; 'and, instead of threatening, I am content to reason with you. I am malicious because I am miserable; am I not shunned and hated by all mankind? You, my creator, would tear me to pieces, and triumph; remember that, and tell me why I should pity man more than he pities me? You would not call it murder.' (102)

The reason the monster is so horrifying is not just his actions, but also the fact that he is the conscience of nature. He tells Frankenstein that his treatment of humans is the same given to him. However, Frankenstein does not consider his actions as the same as the monster's.

The monster is the combination of human thoughts and nature. Paul Outka calls this the organic sublime. In his work, "Posthuman/Post-natural: Ecocriticism and the Sublime in Mary Shelley's Frankenstein," he writes:

> Mary Shelley insistently proffers what I have called the organic sublime, in which subjectivity and materiality are fused. Rather than resolving as an absolute division, the profound instability between self and world that marks the initial moment of the sublime collapses altogether in the (putatively) horrifying monster. (Outka 38)

The answer to the present dichotomy lies within the monster. As Outka comments on, the self and the world collapse together in him. This collapse does not create a new category of humanity/nature, but instead forever mixes them together into one single category. I referred to it as the human natural, but they are created on the same concept. Outka ends his essay by saying that, "We still identify ourselves with Victor and nature with his beloved Alps, still hear the creature's pleas and threats as if they were not our own" (45). It is easy to see only the ugly exterior of the monster, the thing created and abhorred by Victor. But we must instead see this exterior as the distinct human fear of admission that we too, are nature. The monster's existence in the story is supernatural and horrifying, because it is impossible in the current dichotomy of life. The answer lies in listening to the monster, because he is a part of us.

If we do not give the monster's voice an audience, he will fight back. This is to say, the reason we should care about the dichotomy of nature/ humanity is because our existence depends on its dissolution. The monster is a physical representation of the human natural when it is artificially created with the dichotomy still intact. In the story, he is impervious to natural extremities. After the murder of Elizabeth, the monster taunts Frankenstein, "Follow me; I seek the everlasting ices of the north, where you will feel the misery of cold and frost, to which I am impassive" (147). In the struggle between nature and man's need to dominate it, nature is still the stronger. To continue as we have, making nature separate from humanity, is to assure mutual destruction. The dichotomy is a monster of our creation and in order to dissolve it, we must first acknowledge the wrongness of it. Then, we must consider nature as we consider all humani- ty, important and deserving of respect and care. As Bruno Latour writes in his essay "What Is To Be Done? Political Ecology!" he asks for this conces- sion; that "the question of democracy be extended to nonhumans" (Latour 232). It does not matter if we call it organic sublime or the human natural, but the dichotomy must dissolve if we are to extend democracy to all. In his last moments, Frankenstein says, "I created a rational creature, and was bound towards him, to assure, as far as was in my power, his happiness and well-being. This was my duty; but there was another still paramount to that. My duties towards my fellow-creatures" (156). Frankenstein cared more for his own fellow creatures, because the monster was other. But if Frankenstein believed in the human natural, believed that nature outside of humans deserves the same democracy, there would have been no mur- ders in the first place. We need to reevaluate our origin story, because we are all of the same clay. We need to realize that there is no unnaturalness in nature and we are included in that.

Works Cited

Cronon, William. "The Trouble with Wilderness; or, Getting Back to the Wrong Nature." Ecocriticism: The Essential Reader. Ed. Ken Hiltner. New York: Routledge, 2015. 102-119. Print.

Kingsolver, Barbara. "High Tide in Tucson." The Norton Book of Nature Writing. Ed. Robert Finch and John Elder. W.W. Norton and Company, 2002. 1068-1078. Print.

Latour, Bruno. "What is to be Done? Political Ecology!" Ecocriticism: The Essential Reader. Ed. Ken Hiltner. New York: Routledge, 2015. 232-236. Print.

Mortan, Timothy. "Frankenstein and Ecocriticism." The Cambridge Companion to Frankenstein. Ed. Andrew Smith. United Kingdom: University Printing House, 2016. 143-157. Print.

Outka, Paul. "Posthuman/Postnatural: Ecocriticism and the Sublime in Mary Shelley's Frankenstein." Environmental Criticism for the Twenty-First Century. Ed. Stephanie LeMenager, Teresa Shewry, and Ken Hiltner. New York: Routledge, 2011. 31-48. Print.

Shelley, Mary. Frankenstein. New York: W.W. Nortan & Company, 2012. Print.

Snyder, Gary. "The Place, The Region, The Commons" Ecocriticism: The Essential Reader. Ed. Ken Hiltner. New York: Routledge, 2015. 70-76. Print.

White Jr, Lynn. "The Historical Roots of Our Ecologic Crisis." Ecocriticism: The Essential Reader. Ed. Ken Hiltner. New York: Routledge, 2015. 39-46. Print.

The Holy Bible, King James Version. Cambridge Edition: 1769; King James Bible Online, 2017. www.kingjamesbibleonline.org.